foreword

A classic coffee cake is a wonderful, leisurely invitation to sit down and linger—something we should all do more often! A charming coziness surrounds this kind of easy baking, whether it's an old-fashioned streusel or a lovely Bundt cake. Add a cup of coffee (or tea or hot chocolate), and revel in the rightness of the world.

Sharing an ambrosial slice of heaven with a favourite person—or three—makes the pause even sweeter. A half hour with a girlfriend, an afternoon snack with the kids or a work break with a pal gives you time to catch up. Or wrap one as a gift—any new mother, neighbour or friend would love one of these delicious treats, chosen from our Company's Coming library. The recipes are easy; the only hard part will be choosing which of these coffee cake classics to enjoy first.

Jean Paré

sour cream coffee cake

A loaf pan delivers a small batch of goodies—ideal when you don't want leftovers. You can also double the recipe and bake it in a greased, 9 x 9 inch (22 x 22 cm) pan, following the directions below.

Butter (or hard margarine), softened	1/4 cup	60 mL
Granulated sugar	1/2 cup	125 mL
Large egg	1	1
Light sour cream	1/2 cup	125 mL
Vanilla extract	1/2 tsp.	2 mL
All-purpose flour	1 cup	250 mL
Baking powder	1/2 tsp.	2 mL
Baking soda	1/2 tsp.	2 mL
Salt	1/8 tsp.	0.5 mL
CINNAMON NUT TOPPING		
Brown sugar, packed	1/4 cup	60 mL
Finely chopped walnuts (or pecans)	1 tbsp.	30 mL
Ground cinnamon	1/2 tsp.	2 mL

Beat butter and sugar in medium bowl until light and creamy. Add egg. Beat well. Add sour cream and vanilla. Beat.

Combine next 4 ingredients in small bowl. Add to butter mixture. Stir. Spread half of batter evenly in greased 9 x 5 x 3 inch (22 x 12.5 x 7.5 cm) loaf pan.

Cinnamon Nut Topping: Combine all 3 ingredients in small bowl. Sprinkle half over batter in pan. Drop remaining batter by tablespoonfuls over topping. Spread evenly. Sprinkle with remaining topping. Bake in 350°F (175°C) oven for about 30 minutes, until wooden pick inserted in centre comes out clean. Cuts into 6 pieces.

1 piece: 306 Calories; 12.3 g Total Fat (3.9 g Mono, 1.7 g Poly, 7.3 g Sat); 62 mg Cholesterol; 45 g Carbohydrate; 1 g Fibre; 4 g Protein; 281 mg Sodium

coffee streusel cake

Instant granules make this a coffee cake in more ways than one—not only does this moist treat go well with your favourite cup of java, but it's infused with a lovely coffee flavour.

COCONUT STREUSEL

Brown sugar, packed	3/4 cup	175 mL
All-purpose flour	1/3 cup	75 mL
Chopped walnuts	1/3 cup	75 mL
Medium, unsweetened coconut	1/3 cup	75 mL
Ground cinnamon	1 tsp.	5 mL
Hard margarine (or butter), softened	1/4 cup	60 mL

COFFEE CAKE

Hard margarine (or butter), softened	1/2 cup	125 mL
Granulated sugar	3/4 cup	175 mL
Large eggs	2	2
Milk	1/2 cup	125 mL
Instant coffee granules	1 tbsp.	15 mL
Vanilla extract	1 tsp.	5 mL
All-purpose flour	1 1/2 cups	375 mL
Chopped walnuts	2/3 cup	150 mL
Baking powder	1 tbsp.	15 mL
Ground cinnamon	1 tsp.	5 mL
Ground nutmeg	1/2 tsp.	2 mL

Coconut Streusel: Combine first 5 ingredients in medium bowl. Cut in margarine until mixture resembles coarse crumbs. Set aside.

Coffee Cake: Beat margarine and sugar in large bowl until light and creamy. Add eggs, 1 at a time, beating well after each addition.

Combine next 3 ingredients in small bowl. Add to margarine mixture. Stir.

Combine remaining 5 ingredients in separate small bowl. Add to margarine mixture. Stir well. Spread 1/3 of batter evenly in greased 8 x 8 inch (20 x 20 cm) pan. Sprinkle 1/3 of streusel mixture over batter. Repeat 2 more times with remaining batter and streusel mixture. Bake in 350°F (175°C) oven for about 40 minutes, until wooden pick inserted in centre comes out clean. Cuts into 16 pieces.

1 piece: 297 Calories; 16.3 g Total Fat (7.4 g Mono, 4.3 g Poly, 3.7 g Sat); 27 mg Cholesterol; 35 g Carbohydrate; 1 g Fibre; 4 g Protein; 194 mg Sodium

peaches and cream cake

Juicy peaches give this cake an almost creamy texture; serve with extra peach slices and whipped cream to enhance the point. You can substitute the same size of coconut cream pudding powder (not instant) for the vanilla.

Large egg	1	1
All-purpose flour	1 cup	250 mL
Milk	2/3 cup	150 mL
Box of vanilla pudding powder (not instant), 6-serving size	1	1
Hard margarine (or butter), softened	3 tbsp.	50 mL
Baking powder	1 tsp.	5 mL
Salt	1/2 tsp.	2 mL
Can of sliced peaches in juice, drained and juice reserved	14 oz.	398 mL
Cream cheese, softened	8 oz.	250 g
Granulated sugar	1/2 cup	125 mL
Reserved peach juice	3 tbsp.	50 mL
Granulated sugar	2 tbsp.	30 mL
Ground cinnamon	1 tbsp.	15 mL

Beat first 7 ingredients in large bowl until smooth. Spread evenly in greased 8 x 8 inch (20 x 20 cm) pan.

Arrange peach slices over batter.

Beat next 3 ingredients in medium bowl until smooth. Drop by tablespoonfuls over peach slices. Spread evenly.

Combine second amount of sugar and cinnamon in small cup. Sprinkle over cream cheese mixture. Bake in 350°F (175°C) oven for 60 to 70 minutes, until wooden pick inserted in centre comes out clean. Cuts into 16 pieces.

1 piece: 193 Calories; 8.2 g Total Fat (3.1 g Mono, 0.5 g Poly, 4.1 g Sat); 31 mg Cholesterol; 28 g Carbohydrate; 1 g Fibre; 3 g Protein; 252 mg Sodium

oatmeal cake

To ensure the best results with any baking, choose the correct pan size as indicated in the recipe. If you plan to experiment with slightly different sizes, remember to leave room for the batter to rise.

Boiling water	1 cup	250 mL
Quick-cooking rolled oats	1 cup	250 mL
Large eggs	2	2
Granulated sugar	1 cup	250 mL
Cooking oil	1/2 cup	125 mL
Vanilla extract	1 tsp.	5 mL
All-purpose flour	1 1/3 cups	325 mL
Baking soda	1 1/2 tsp.	7 mL
Ground cinnamon	1 tsp.	5 mL
Salt	1/2 tsp.	2 mL

NUTTY COCONUT TOPPING

Brown sugar, packed	2/3 cup	150 mL
Chopped pecans (or walnuts)	1/2 cup	125 mL
Medium unsweetened coconut	1/2 cup	125 mL
Hard margarine (or butter)	1/4 cup	60 mL
	1/4 cup	60 mL
Half-and-half cream (or milk)	2 tbsp.	30 mL

Pour boiling water over rolled oats in small bowl. Let stand, uncovered, for 20 minutes.

Beat eggs in large bowl until frothy. Add sugar. Beat. Add cooking oil and vanilla. Beat until well combined.

Combine next 4 ingredients in separate small bowl. Add flour mixture to egg mixture in 3 additions, alternating with oatmeal mixture in 2 additions, beginning and ending with flour mixture. Spread evenly in greased 9 x 9 inch (22 x 22 cm) pan. Bake in 350°F (175°C) oven for about 30 minutes until wooden pick inserted in centre comes out clean.

Nutty Coconut Topping: Combine all 5 ingredients in small saucepan. Heat and stir on medium-low until margarine is melted and brown sugar is dissolved. Do not boil. Makes about 1 cup (250 mL) topping. Spread over cake. Bake for 5 to 7 minutes, until top is bubbling. Cuts into 16 pieces.

1 piece: 302 Calories; 16.2 g Total Fat (8.4 g Mono, 3.4 g Poly, 3.5 g Sat); 28 mg Cholesterol; 37 g Carbohydrate; 1 g Fibre; 3 g Protein; 244 mg Sodium

fig and macadamia cake

It's a good idea to let your eggs stand on the counter for 15 minutes before you use them in baking. If they're too cold, they won't combine well with the softened butter, ruining the cake's texture.

Chopped dried figs	1 1/2 cups	375 mL
Water	1 1/2 cups	375 mL
Baking soda	1 tsp.	5 mL
Butter (or hard margarine), softened	1/2 cup	125 mL
Granulated sugar	1 cup	250 mL
Large eggs	3	3
All-purpose flour	1 1/2 cups	375 mL
Baking powder	2 tsp.	10 mL
Finely chopped raw macadamia nuts, toasted (see Tip, page 64)	2/3 cup	150 mL
Icing (confectioner's) sugar	1 tbsp.	15 mL

Line bottom of greased 9 x 9 inch (22 x 22 cm) pan with waxed paper. Combine figs and water in medium saucepan. Bring to a boil. Remove from heat. Add baking soda. Stir. Let stand, covered, for 5 minutes. Process in blender or food processor until smooth (see Safety Tip). Set aside.

Beat butter and granulated sugar in medium bowl until light and creamy. Add eggs, 1 at a time, beating well after each addition.

Combine flour and baking powder in small bowl. Add to butter mixture. Stir. Add fig mixture. Stir until well combined.

Add macadamia nuts. Stir. Spread in prepared pan. Bake in 350°F (175°C) oven for about 1 hour, until wooden pick inserted in centre comes out clean. Let stand in pan on wire rack for 10 minutes. Run knife around inside edges of pan to loosen cake before removing to wire rack to cool.

Dust with icing sugar. Cuts into 12 pieces.

1 piece: 325 Calories; 15.6 g Total Fat (7.5 g Mono, 0.7 g Poly, 6.4 g Sat); 76 mg Cholesterol; 45 g Carbohydrate; 3 g Fibre; 5 g Protein; 270 mg Sodium

Safety Tip: Follow manufacturer's instructions for processing hot liquids.

cherry treasure snack cake

Some lucky kid will uncover the single whole cherry "buried" in this cake. The chopped cherries and chocolate bits embedded in the rest of the cake are more than adequate consolation prizes.

Hard margarine (or butter), softened	1/2 cup	125 mL
Granulated sugar	1 cup	250 mL
Large eggs	2	2
Chopped maraschino cherries	1/4 cup	60 mL
Semi-sweet chocolate baking square, grated	1 oz.	28 g
Vanilla extract	1 tsp.	5 mL
Maraschino cherry	1	1
All-purpose flour	1 1/2 cups	375 mL
Baking powder	1 1/2 tsp.	7 mL
Salt	1/4 tsp.	1 mL
Maraschino cherry syrup	1/4 cup	60 mL
Icing (confectioner's) sugar	1 tbsp.	15 mL

Beat margarine and granulated sugar in large bowl until light and creamy. Add eggs, 1 at a time, beating well after each addition.

Add next 4 ingredients. Stir.

Combine next 3 ingredients in small bowl. Add to margarine mixture in 3 additions, alternating with cherry syrup in 2 additions, beginning and ending with flour mixture. Spread evenly in greased 9 x 9 inch (22 x 22 cm) pan. Bake in 350°F (175°C) oven for about 35 minutes, until wooden pick inserted in centre comes out clean. Let stand in pan on wire rack until cool.

Dust each serving with icing sugar. Cuts into 9 pieces.

1 piece: 318 Calories; 13.0 g Total Fat (7.8 g Mono, 1.3 g Poly, 3.1 g Sat); 48 mg Cholesterol; 47 g Carbohydrate; 1 g Fibre; 4 g Protein; 269 mg Sodium

lazy daisy cake

The first part of this recipe is for a basic shortcake. Add whipped cream and fruit and you'll have a lovely dessert. Or go for broke and add the fabulous coconut topping. Leftovers? Impossible!

Large eggs	2	2
Granulated sugar	1 cup	250 mL
Vanilla extract	1 tsp.	5 mL
All-purpose flour	1 cup	250 mL
Baking powder	1 tsp.	5 mL
Salt	1/2 tsp.	2 mL
Milk	1/2 cup	125 mL
Hard margarine (or butter)	1 tbsp.	15 mL
FLAKED COCONUT TOPPING		
Brown sugar, packed	1/2 cup	125 mL
Hard margarine (or butter)	3 tbsp.	50 mL
Half-and-half cream (or milk)	2 tbsp.	30 mL
Flaked coconut	1/2 cup	125 mL

Beat eggs in medium bowl until frothy. Add sugar, 2 tbsp. (30 mL) at a time, beating constantly until thickened. Add vanilla. Stir.

Combine next 3 ingredients in small bowl. Add to egg mixture. Stir.

Combine milk and margarine in small heavy saucepan. Heat and stir on medium until margarine is melted. Add to flour mixture. Stir well. Spread evenly in greased 9 x 9 inch (22 x 22 cm) pan. Bake in 350°F (175°C) oven for 25 to 30 minutes, until wooden pick inserted in centre comes out clean.

Flaked Coconut Topping: Combine first 3 ingredients in medium saucepan. Bring to a rolling boil on medium-high, stirring occasionally. Remove from heat.

Add coconut. Stir. Spread evenly over warm cake. Bake for about 3 minutes until top is bubbling. Let stand in pan on wire rack until cool. Cuts into 12 pieces.

1 piece: 226 Calories; 7.7 g Total Fat (3.1 g Mono, 0.6 g Poly, 3.6 g Sat); 37 mg Cholesterol; 37 g Carbohydrate; 1 g Fibre; 3 g Protein; 198 mg Sodium

fat-free chocolate cake

Use a paper doily, snowflake or even several simple stars or hearts to create a pattern for a dusting of icing sugar. If you're using smaller pattern pieces, roll a small piece of tape and attach it to the paper so you can lift it up and off without disturbing the icing sugar.

All-purpose flour	1 1/4 cups	300 mL
Granulated sugar	1 cup	250 mL
Cocoa, sifted if lumpy	1/2 cup	125 mL
Cornstarch	1/4 cup	60 mL
Baking soda	1/2 tsp.	2 mL
Salt	1/2 tsp.	2 mL
Egg whites (large)	4	4
Water	1 cup	250 mL
Dark corn syrup	1/2 cup	125 mL

Combine first 6 ingredients in medium bowl. Make a well in centre.

Whisk remaining 3 ingredients in separate medium bowl. Add to well. Stir until smooth. Spread evenly in greased 9 x 9 inch (22 x 22 cm) pan. Bake in 350°F (175°C) oven for about 30 minutes, until wooden pick inserted in centre comes out clean. Cuts into 16 pieces.

1 piece: 138 Calories; 0.3 g Total Fat (0.1 g Mono, trace Poly, 0.1 g Sat); 0 mg Cholesterol; 33 g Carbohydrate; 2 g Fibre; 3 g Protein; 149 mg Sodium

raspberry coffee cake

A favourite babysitter or teacher will happily accept a batch of these raspberry delights. You can use fresh raspberries too. As with most quick-bread recipes, this one can be easily doubled.

All-purpose flour	1 2/3 cups	400 mL
Granulated sugar	3/4 cup	175 mL
Baking powder	1 tbsp.	15 mL
Salt	1/4 tsp.	1 mL
Cold hard margarine (or butter), cut up	1/3 cup	75 mL
Large egg, fork-beaten	1	1
Milk	1 cup	250 mL
Vanilla extract	1 tsp.	5 mL
Frozen whole raspberries	1 1/2 cups	375 mL
Brown sugar, packed	1/2 cup	125 mL
Ground cinnamon	3/4 tsp.	4 mL

Combine first 4 ingredients in large bowl. Cut in margarine until mixture resembles coarse crumbs. Make a well in centre.

Add next 3 ingredients to well. Stir until just moistened. Spread evenly in greased 9 x 9 inch (22 x 22 cm) pan. Sprinkle with raspberries.

Combine brown sugar and cinnamon in small bowl. Sprinkle over raspberries. Bake in 350°F (175°C) oven for about 50 minutes, until wooden pick inserted in centre comes out clean. Cuts into 9 pieces.

1 piece: 303 Calories; 8.4 g Total Fat (5.0 g Mono, 1.0 g Poly, 1.9 g Sat); 25 mg Cholesterol; 54 g Carbohydrate; 2 g Fibre; 4 g Protein; 300 mg Sodium

carrot coffee cake

By using your food processor's shredder disk to grate the carrots, you'll get this cake into the oven even faster. Have a bowl of freshly whipped cream on hand so guests can help themselves.

Large eggs	3	3
Box of yellow cake mix (2 layer size)	1	1
Plain yogurt	1 cup	250 mL
Frozen concentrated orange juice, thawed	1/4 cup	60 mL
Ground cinnamon	1 tsp.	5 mL
Finely grated carrot	2 cups	500 mL
Chopped walnuts	1 cup	250 mL
Brown sugar, packed	1/2 cup	125 mL
Grated orange zest	2 tsp.	10 mL
Ground cinnamon	1/2 tsp.	2 mL
Ground cloves	1/4 tsp.	1 mL

Combine first 5 ingredients in large bowl. Beat for about 2 minutes until smooth.

Add carrot. Mix well. Spread half of batter evenly in greased 9 x 13 inch (22 x 33 cm) pan.

Combine remaining 5 ingredients in small bowl. Sprinkle half of walnut mixture over batter. Drop remaining batter by tablespoonfuls over top. Smooth gently. Sprinkle with remaining walnut mixture. Bake in 350°F (175°C) oven for about 40 minutes, until wooden pick inserted in centre comes out clean. Cuts into 15 pieces.

1 piece: 275 Calories; 10.4 g Total Fat (3.3 g Mono, 5.0 g Poly, 1.4 g Sat); 45 mg Cholesterol; 41 g Carbohydrate; 1 g Fibre; 6 g Protein; 263 mg Sodium

old-fashioned coffee cake

Try this once with cherry pie filling, and then experiment with variations—blueberry, apple or your family's favourite. Vanilla ice cream makes a nice accompaniment, especially if the cake's still warm from the oven.

All-purpose flour	2 cups	500 mL
Granulated sugar	1 cup	250 mL
Baking powder	2 tsp.	10 mL
Salt	1/4 tsp.	1 mL
Cold butter (or hard margarine), cut up	1/2 cup	125 mL
Large egg, fork-beaten	1	1
Milk	3/4 cup	175 mL
Can of cherry pie filling	19 oz.	540 mL
BROWN SUGAR CRUMBLE		
All-purpose flour	1 cup	250 mL
Brown sugar, packed	1 cup	250 mL
Cold butter (or hard margarine), cut up	1/2 cup	125 mL

Combine first 4 ingredients in large bowl. Cut in butter until mixture resembles coarse crumbs. Make a well in centre.

Add egg and milk to well. Stir until just moistened. Spread evenly in greased 9 x 13 inch (22 x 33 cm) baking pan.

Spread pie filling over top.

Brown Sugar Crumble: Combine flour and brown sugar in small bowl. Cut in butter until mixture resembles coarse crumbs. Sprinkle over pie filling. Bake in 375°F (190°C) oven for about 40 minutes, until top is golden and filling is bubbling. Let stand on wire rack for 10 minutes. Cuts into 15 pieces.

1 piece: 380 Calories; 13.8 g Total Fat (4.0 g Mono, 0.7 g Poly, 8.3 g Sat); 50 mg Cholesterol; 62 g Carbohydrate; 1 g Fibre; 4 g Protein; 242 mg Sodium

date cake

It's a good idea to grease pans and tins, even if they're non-stick. A coating of fat allows the sides of your baking to crisp, and makes clean up a snap. We use cooking spray in our test kitchen.

Chopped pitted dates	1 1/2 cups	375 mL
Baking soda	1 1/2 tsp.	7 mL
Boiling water	1 1/2 cups	375 mL
Hard margarine (or butter), softened	3/4 cup	175 mL
Brown sugar, packed	1 cup	250 mL
Granulated sugar	1/2 cup	125 mL
Large eggs	2	2
Vanilla extract	1 tsp.	5 mL
All-purpose flour	2 1/2 cups	625 mL
Baking powder	1 1/2 tsp.	7 mL
Salt	1/2 tsp.	2 mL

FINE COCONUT TOPPING

Brown sugar, packed	1 cup	250 mL
Hard margarine (or butter)	1/3 cup	75 mL
Half-and-half cream (or milk)	3 tbsp.	50 mL
Fine coconut	1 cup	250 mL

Put dates into medium bowl. Sprinkle with baking soda. Pour boiling water over top. Let stand until cool. Stir.

Beat next 3 ingredients in large bowl until light and creamy. Add eggs, 1 at a time, beating well after each addition. Add vanilla. Beat.

Combine remaining 3 ingredients in small bowl. Add to margarine mixture in 3 additions, alternating with date mixture in 2 additions, beginning and ending with flour mixture. Spread evenly in greased 9 x 13 inch (22 x 33 cm) pan. Bake in 325°F (160°C) oven for 40 to 50 minutes, until wooden pick inserted in centre comes out clean.

Fine Coconut Topping: Combine first 3 ingredients in medium saucepan. Bring to a rolling boil on medium-high, stirring occasionally. Remove from heat.

Add coconut. Stir. Spread evenly over warm cake. Bake for about 3 minutes until top is bubbling. Let stand in pan on wire rack until cool. Cuts into 18 pieces.

1 piece: 365 Calories; 15.4 g Total Fat (7.7 g Mono, 1.3 g Poly, 5.5 g Sat); 24 mg Cholesterol; 56 g Carbohydrate; 2 g Fibre; 3 g Protein; 347 mg Sodium

orange oatmeal cake

A foil-wrapped pan of this orange-scented delight is easily reheated.

Boiling water	1 1/4 cups	300 mL
Quick-cooking rolled oats	1 cup	250 mL
All-purpose flour	1 3/4 cups	425 mL
Baking powder	1 tsp.	5 mL
Baking soda	1 tsp.	5 mL
Ground cinnamon	1/2 tsp.	2 mL
Salt	1/2 tsp.	2 mL
Hard margarine (or butter), softened	1/2 cup	125 mL
Granulated sugar	1 cup	250 mL
Brown sugar, packed	1/2 cup	125 mL
Large eggs	2	2
Frozen concentrated orange juice, thawed	1/4 cup	60 mL
Vanilla extract	1 tsp.	5 mL

ORANGE COCONUT TOPPING

Brown sugar, packed	1/2 cup	125 mL
Hard margarine (or butter)	1/4 cup	60 mL
Frozen concentrated orange juice, thawed	2 tbsp.	30 mL
Flaked coconut	1 cup	250 mL
Chopped walnuts	1/2 cup	125 mL

Pour boiling water over rolled oats in small bowl. Set aside.

Combine next 5 ingredients in separate small bowl.

Beat next 3 ingredients in large bowl until light and creamy. Add eggs, 1 at a time, beating well after each addition. Add concentrated orange juice and vanilla. Mix. Add flour mixture in 3 additions, alternating with rolled oat mixture in 2 additions, beginning and ending with flour mixture. Stir until just moistened. Spread evenly in greased 9 x 13 inch (22 x 33 cm) pan. Bake in 350°F (175°C) oven for about 40 minutes, until wooden pick inserted in centre comes out clean.

Orange Coconut Topping: Combine first 3 ingredients in small saucepan. Heat and stir until boiling. Boil for 1 minute.

Add coconut and walnuts. Stir. Spoon over hot cake. Broil on top rack in oven until topping is golden. Cuts into 16 pieces.

1 piece: 348 Calories; 16.7 g Total Fat (7.1 g Mono, 2.8 g Poly, 5.8 g Sat); 27 mg Cholesterol; 47 g Carbohydrate; 2 g Fibre; 4 g Protein; 295 mg Sodium

apple streusel coffee cake

For a special touch, save a bit of the Spicy Streusel to sprinkle on a bowl of freshly whipped cream and serve with fruit slices.

White vinegar	2 tbsp.	30 mL
Milk, approximately	1 3/4 cups	425 mL
Butter (or hard margarine), softened	3/4 cup	175 mL
Granulated sugar	1 3/4 cups	425 mL
Large eggs	2	2
Vanilla extract	1 tsp.	5 mL
All-purpose flour	3 cups	750 mL
Baking powder	2 tsp.	10 mL
Baking soda	1 tsp.	5 mL
Salt	1/4 tsp.	1 mL
Medium peeled cooking apples (such as McIntosh), thinly sliced	2	2

SPICY STREUSEL

Granulated sugar	2/3 cup	150 mL
All-purpose flour	1/2 cup	125 mL
Ground cinnamon	2 tsp.	10 mL
Ground nutmeg	1/4 tsp.	1 mL
Cold butter (or hard margarine), cut up	1/4 cup	60 mL

Measure vinegar into 2 cup (500 mL) liquid measure. Add milk to equal 1 3/4 cups (425 mL). Let stand for 1 minute.

Beat butter and sugar in large bowl until light and creamy. Add eggs, 1 at a time, beating well after each addition. Add vanilla. Stir.

Combine next 4 ingredients in medium bowl. Add to butter mixture in 4 additions, alternating with milk mixture in 3 additions, beginning and ending with flour mixture. Spread half of batter evenly in greased 9 x 13 inch (22 x 33 cm) pan.

Arrange apple in single layer over batter.

Spicy Streusel: Combine first 4 ingredients in small bowl. Cut in butter until mixture resembles coarse crumbs. Sprinkle 1/2 cup (125 mL) streusel over apples. Spread remaining batter evenly over streusel. Sprinkle with remaining streusel. Bake in 350°F (175°C) oven for about 55 minutes, until wooden pick inserted in centre comes out clean. Cuts into 15 pieces.

1 piece: 394 Calories; 14.0 g Total Fat (4.1 g Mono, 0.7 g Poly, 8.6 g Sat); 65 mg Cholesterol; 62 g Carbohydrate; 1 g Fibre; 5 g Protein; 332 mg Sodium

lemon loaf

These slices of lemony heaven can brighten even the coldest, gloomiest day. While they're irresistible when fresh from the oven, loaves that are cut once they've cooled for several hours—or even overnight—crumble less.

Hard margarine (or butter), softened	1/2 cup	125 mL
Granulated sugar	1 cup	250 mL
Large eggs	2	2
Milk	1/2 cup	125 mL
All-purpose flour	1 1/2 cups	375 mL
Grated lemon zest (see Tip, page 64)	1 tbsp.	15 mL
Baking powder	1 tsp.	5 mL
Salt	1/2 tsp.	2 mL
LEMON GLAZE		
Lemon juice	1/3 cup	75 mL
Granulated sugar	1/4 cup	60 mL

Beat margarine and sugar in large bowl until light and creamy. Add eggs, 1 at a time, beating well after each addition. Add milk. Beat well.

Combine next 4 ingredients in small bowl. Add to margarine mixture. Stir until just moistened. Spread evenly in greased 9 x 5 x 3 inch (22 x 12.5 x 7.5 cm) loaf pan. Bake in 350°F (175°C) oven for about 60 minutes, until wooden pick inserted in centre comes out clean.

Lemon Glaze: Combine lemon juice and sugar in small saucepan. Heat and stir on medium until sugar is dissolved. Spoon evenly over hot loaf. Let stand in pan on wire rack for 10 minutes before removing to wire rack to cool. Cuts into 16 slices.

1 slice: 177 Calories; 6.9 g Total Fat (4.2 g Mono, 0.7 g Poly, 1.5 g Sat); 27 mg Cholesterol; 27 g Carbohydrate; trace Fibre; 2 g Protein; 180 mg Sodium

granola banana bread

For a low-cal version, use 2 cups (500 mL) mashed banana, cut the butter in half and reduce the sugar to 1/3 cup (75 mL). But if calories are no object, toss a handful of chopped chocolate kisses into the batter.

All-purpose flour	2 cups	500 mL
Granola	1/2 cup	125 mL
Baking soda	1 tsp.	5 mL
Salt	1/2 tsp.	2 mL
Butter (or hard margarine), softened	1/2 cup	125 mL
Granulated sugar	1 cup	250 mL
Large eggs	2	2
Mashed overripe banana (about 3 medium)	1 1/2 cups	375 mL
Chopped walnuts	1/2 cup	125 mL
Dark raisins	1/2 cup	125 mL
Lemon juice	1 tbsp.	15 mL
Vanilla extract	1 tsp.	5 mL

Combine first 4 ingredients in large bowl. Make a well in centre.

Beat butter and sugar in medium bowl until light and creamy. Add eggs 1 at a time, beating well after each addition.

Add remaining 5 ingredients. Stir. Add to well. Stir until just moistened. Spread evenly in greased 9 x 5 x 3 inch (22 x 12.5 x 7.5 cm) loaf pan. Bake in 350°F (175°C) oven for 60 to 70 minutes, until wooden pick inserted in centre comes out clean. Let stand in pan on wire rack for 10 minutes before removing to wire rack to cool. Cuts into 16 slices.

1 slice: 196 Calories; 7.0 g Total Fat (2.0 g Mono, 0.4 g Poly, 4.1 g Sat); 43 mg Cholesterol; 31 g Carbohydrate; 1 g Fibre; 3 g Protein; 225 mg Sodium

orange loaf

Freezing quick breads is easy. Just wrap them in plastic and then in aluminum foil and freeze for up to two months. Let them thaw overnight and if a glaze or icing is required, add it just before serving.

Large egg	1	1
Granulated sugar	1 cup	250 mL
Cooking oil	1/4 cup	60 mL
Vanilla extract	1 tsp.	5 mL
Orange juice	1 cup	250 mL
Grated orange zest (see Tip, page 64)	3 tbsp.	50 mL
All-purpose flour	2 1/2 cups	625 mL
Baking powder	1 tbsp.	15 mL
Salt	1/2 tsp.	2 mL

Beat first 4 ingredients in large bowl. Add orange juice and zest. Stir until well combined.

Combine remaining 3 ingredients in medium bowl. Add to orange mixture. Stir until just moistened. Spread evenly in greased 9 x 5 x 3 inch (22 x 12.5 x 7.5 cm) loaf pan. Bake in 350°F (175°C) oven for about 45 minutes, until wooden pick inserted in centre comes out clean. Let stand in pan on wire rack for 10 minutes before removing to wire rack to cool. Cuts into 16 slices.

1 slice: 172 Calories; 4.2 g Total Fat (2.3 g Mono, 1.2 g Poly, 0.4 g Sat); 13 mg Cholesterol; 31 g Carbohydrate; 1 g Fibre; 3 g Protein; 82 mg Sodium

cranberry walnut loaf

A word (or three!) about mixing quick breads: don't overdo it! Stir until the flour is moist, but not smooth. Lumpy batter will produce light and tender baking, such as this tart and tasty loaf.

All-purpose flour	2 cups	500 mL
Brown sugar, packed	3/4 cup	175 mL
Baking powder	1 1/2 tsp.	7 mL
Salt	1 tsp.	5 mL
Large eggs	2	2
Buttermilk (or soured milk, see Tip, page 64)	3/4 cup	175 mL
Butter (or hard margarine), melted	1/2 cup	125 mL
Vanilla extract	1 1/2 tsp.	7 mL
Grated lemon zest	1 tsp.	5 mL
Dried cranberries, chopped	1 cup	250 mL
WALNUT TOPPING		
Finely chopped walnuts	1/4 cup	60 mL
Brown sugar, packed	2 tbsp.	30 mL
Ground cinnamon	1/4 tsp.	1 mL

Combine first 4 ingredients in large bowl. Make a well in centre.

Combine next 5 ingredients in medium bowl. Add to well. Add cranberries. Stir until just moistened. Spread evenly in greased 9 x 5 x 3 inch (22 x 12.5 x 7.5 cm) loaf pan.

Walnut Topping: Combine all 3 ingredients in small bowl. Sprinkle over batter. Bake in 350°F (175°C) oven for 45 to 50 minutes, until wooden pick inserted in centre comes out clean. Let stand in pan on wire rack for 10 minutes before removing to wire rack to cool. Cuts into 16 slices.

1 slice: 202 Calories; 8.2 g Total Fat (2.3 g Mono, 1.2 g Poly, 4.2 g Sat); 44 mg Cholesterol; 29 g Carbohydrate; 2 g Fibre; 4 g Protein; 271 mg Sodium

fruit tea loaf

OK, not every quick bread needs to be a coffee cake. Tea lovers will enjoy this loaf infused with their favourite beverage. To prepare, pour the required amount of boiling water over a teabag and allow it to steep.

Granulated sugar	1 cup	250 mL
Strong, prepared tea	1 cup	250 mL
Chopped, mixed glazed fruit	1/2 cup	125 mL
Raisins	1/2 cup	125 mL
Hard margarine (or butter)	1/4 cup	60 mL
Large eggs	2	2
Vanilla extract	1 tsp.	5 mL
All-purpose flour	2 1/4 cups	550 mL
Baking powder	2 tsp.	10 mL
Salt	1/2 tsp.	2 mL

Combine first 5 ingredients in large saucepan on medium-low. Bring to a boil, stirring occasionally. Reduce heat to medium-low. Simmer, uncovered, for 3 minutes, stirring occasionally. Cool slightly.

Beat eggs and vanilla with fork in small cup. Add to fruit mixture. Stir.

Combine remaining 3 ingredients in small bowl. Add to fruit mixture. Stir until just moistened. Spread evenly in greased 9 x 5 x 3 inch (22 x 12.5 x 7.5 cm) loaf pan. Bake in 350°F (175°C) oven for about 50 minutes, until wooden pick inserted in centre comes out clean. Let stand in pan on wire rack for 10 minutes before removing to wire rack to cool. Cuts into 18 slices.

1 slice: 170 Calories; 3.5 g Total Fat (2.0 g Mono, 0.4 g Poly, 0.8 g Sat); 24 mg Cholesterol; 33 g Carbohydrate; 1 g Fibre; 3 g Protein; 151 mg Sodium

almond coffee bread

Bake and freeze this indulgence (before icing it) for a leisurely brunch.

Loaves of frozen white bread dough, covered, thawed in refrigerator overnight	2	2
Chopped, red-glazed cherries	2/3 cup	150 mL
Granulated sugar	1/2 cup	125 mL
Ground cinnamon	1 tsp.	5 mL
Butter (or hard margarine), softened	1/4 cup	60 mL
Large egg, fork-beaten	1	1
Sliced almonds	1/3 cup	75 mL
VANILLA DRIZZLE		
Water	1 tbsp.	15 mL
Vanilla	1/4 tsp.	1 mL
Icing (confectioner's) sugar	1 cup	250 mL

Knead the bread dough portions together. Divide into 3 equal portions. Roll out each portion to 12 inch (30 cm) diameter circle. Set aside.

Combine next 3 ingredients in small bowl. Assemble cake by layering ingredients in greased 12 inch (30 cm) deep-dish pizza pan as follows:

1. 1 dough circle
2. 2 tbsp. (30 mL) butter
3. Half of cherry mixture
4. 1 dough circle
5. Remaining butter
6. Remaining cherry mixture
7. Remaining dough circle

Position 2 to 2 1/2 inch (5 to 6.5 cm) round cookie cutter in centre of top. Mark dough into 16 wedges from outside of cookie cutter to edge of pizza pan. Using sharp knife, cut through marks to bottom. Twist each wedge 5 times in same direction and arc slightly. Cover with greased waxed paper and tea towel. Let stand in oven with light on and door closed for about 1 hour until doubled in size.

Brush with egg. Sprinkle with almonds. Bake in 375°F (190°C) oven for about 30 minutes, until golden brown. Let stand in pan on wire rack for 10 minutes before removing to wire rack to cool.

Vanilla Drizzle: Stir water and vanilla into icing sugar in small bowl until smooth. Add more water if necessary until barely pourable consistency. Drizzle over warm cake. Serve warm or cold. Cuts into 16 wedges.

1 wedge: 263 Calories; 6.6 g Total Fat (1.6 g Mono, 0.4 g Poly, 2.0 g Sat); 21 mg Cholesterol; 46 g Carbohydrate; 3 g Fibre; 8 g Protein; 347 mg Sodium

apricot coffee cake

When you've promised to bring something to a shower or a housewarming, keep this gorgeous cake in mind. It travels well and tastes wonderful. Be prepared to hand out the recipe!

All-purpose flour	1 3/4 cups	425 mL
Granulated sugar	1/3 cup	75 mL
Hard margarine (or butter), cut up	2/3 cup	150 mL
Large egg	1	1
Light cream cheese, softened	8 oz.	250 g
Granulated sugar	1/2 cup	125 mL
Light sour cream	1 cup	250 mL
Almond extract	1 tsp.	5 mL
All-purpose flour	2 tbsp.	30 mL
Baking powder	1/2 tsp.	2 mL
Salt	1/2 tsp.	2 mL
Can of apricot halves in light syrup, drained	14 oz.	398 mL
Sliced almonds	1/3 cup	75 mL

Combine first amounts of flour and sugar in medium bowl. Cut in margarine until mixture resembles coarse crumbs. Reserve 3/4 cup (175 mL) in small cup. Press remaining flour mixture in bottom of greased 9 inch (22 cm) springform pan.

Beat next 3 ingredients in large bowl until smooth. Add sour cream and extract. Beat.

Combine next 3 ingredients in small bowl. Add to cream cheese mixture. Beat. Spread evenly over flour mixture in pan.

Arrange apricot, cut side down, over batter. Sprinkle with reserved flour mixture. Sprinkle with almonds. Bake in 350°F (175°C) oven for about 90 minutes until set and browned. Let stand in pan on wire rack for at least 20 minutes. Serve warm or at room temperature. Cuts into 10 wedges.

1 wedge: 391 Calories; 22.2 g Total Fat (12.4 g Mono, 2.2 g Poly, 7.9 g Sat); 42 mg Cholesterol; 42 g Carbohydrate; 2 g Fibre; 7 g Protein; 482 mg Sodium

apricot butter cake

Here's another apricot cake, but so different and so delicious. It's easy to substitute slices of canned peaches, plums or even a cup (250 mL) of fresh berries for the apricots.

Butter, softened	3/4 cup	175 mL
Granulated sugar	3/4 cup	175 mL
Grated orange zest	2 tsp.	10 mL
Large eggs	3	3
All-purpose flour	1 2/3 cups	400 mL
Baking powder	2 tsp.	10 mL
Salt	1/4 tsp.	1 mL
Milk	1/2 cup	125 mL
Can of apricot halves in light syrup, drained and chopped	14 oz.	398 mL
APRICOT TOPPING		
Unflavoured gelatin	1 tsp.	5 mL
Water	2 tbsp.	30 mL
Apricot jam, warmed and strained	3 tbsp.	50 mL

Line bottom of greased 9 inch (22 cm) springform pan with waxed paper. Beat first 3 ingredients in medium bowl until light and creamy. Add eggs, 1 at a time, beating well after each addition.

Combine next 3 ingredients in small bowl. Add to butter mixture. Add milk. Stir well. Spread evenly in prepared pan.

Sprinkle apricot over top. Bake in 350°F (175°C) oven for about 50 minutes, until top is golden and wooden pick inserted in centre comes out clean. Let stand in pan on wire rack for 10 minutes.

Apricot Topping: Sprinkle gelatin over water in small saucepan. Let stand for 1 minute. Heat and stir on medium-low until gelatin is dissolved.

Add jam. Stir well. Makes about 1/4 cup (60 mL) topping. Brush warm topping over warm cake. Let stand in pan on wire rack until cooled completely. Run knife around inside edge of pan to loosen cake. Cuts into 8 wedges.

1 wedge: 410 Calories; 20.7 g Total Fat (6.1 g Mono, 1.1 g Poly, 12.0 g Sat); 131 mg Cholesterol; 50 g Carbohydrate; 2 g Fibre; 7 g Protein; 392 mg Sodium

lime poppy seed cake

A bowl of fresh, juicy berries splashed with white grape juice or sweet dessert wine would complement this moist cake splendidly.

Milk	1 cup	250 mL
Poppy seeds	3 tbsp.	50 mL
Egg whites (large), room temperature	3	3
Almond extract	1 tsp.	5 mL
Hard margarine (or butter), softened	1 cup	250 mL
Granulated sugar	1 1/4 cups	300 mL
Egg yolks (large)	3	3
Grated lime zest (see Tip, page 64)	1 tbsp.	15 mL
All-purpose flour	2 cups	500 mL
Baking powder	1 tbsp.	15 mL
Salt	1/2 tsp.	2 mL
LIME DRIZZLE		
Hot water	2 tbsp.	30 mL
Icing (confectioner's) sugar	3/4 cup	175 mL
Lime juice	6 tbsp.	100 mL

Fresh berries, for garnish

Combine milk and poppy seeds in small saucepan on medium. Heat and stir until very hot, but not boiling. Cool.

Beat egg whites and extract in medium bowl until stiff peaks form. Set aside.

Beat margarine and sugar in large bowl until light and creamy. Add egg yolks, lime zest and milk mixture. Beat well.

Combine next 3 ingredients in small bowl. Add to margarine mixture. Beat well. Fold egg white mixture into flour mixture until no white streaks remain. Spread evenly in greased 10 inch (25 cm) angel food tube pan or 10 inch (25 cm) springform pan. Bake in 325°F (160°C) oven for about 1 hour, until wooden pick inserted in centre of cake comes out clean. Let stand in pan on wire rack for 10 minutes before removing to serving plate.

Lime Drizzle: Stir hot water into icing sugar in small bowl until smooth. Add lime juice. Stir. Makes about 1 cup (250 mL). Drizzle over hot cake. Let stand until cool.

Garnish with fresh berries. Cuts into 12 wedges.

1 wedge: 384 Calories; 18.8 g Total Fat (11.2 g Mono, 2.6 g Poly, 4.0 g Sat); 55 mg Cholesterol; 50 g Carbohydrate; 1 g Fibre; 5 g Protein; 408 mg Sodium

pecan bundkuchen

Germans and Austrians have a long tradition of baking coffee cakes, called Bundkuchen or Gugelhupf, in elaborate ceramic or cast iron forms. In 1950, an American company created an aluminum form and added a "t" to "Bund" to name the pan for this tasty cake.

PECAN CRUMBLE

Chopped pecans (or walnuts)	3/4 cup	175 mL
Brown sugar, packed	1/3 cup	75 mL
Ground cinnamon	1 tsp.	5 mL

BUNDKUCHEN

Hard margarine (or butter), softened	1/2 cup	125 mL
Granulated sugar	1 1/4 cups	300 mL
Large eggs	2	2
Sour cream	1 cup	250 mL
Vanilla extract	1 tsp.	5 mL
All-purpose flour	1 3/4 cups	425 mL
Baking powder	1 1/2 tsp.	7 mL
Baking soda	1/2 tsp.	2 mL
Salt	1/4 tsp.	1 mL

Pecan Crumble: Combine all 3 ingredients in small bowl. Sprinkle half of pecan mixture into bottom of well-greased 12 cup (3 L) Bundt pan.

Bundkuchen: Beat margarine and sugar in large bowl until light and creamy. Add eggs, 1 at a time, beating well after each addition. Add sour cream and vanilla. Beat.

Combine remaining 4 ingredients in small bowl. Add to margarine mixture. Stir just until moistened. Spread half of batter evenly in prepared pan. Sprinkle with remaining pecan mixture. Drop remaining batter by tablespoonfuls over top. Spread evenly. Bake in 350°F (175°C) oven for about 45 minutes, until wooden pick inserted in centre comes out clean. Let stand in pan on wire rack for 10 minutes before removing to wire rack to cool. Cuts into 16 wedges.

1 wedge: 261 Calories; 12.9 g Total Fat (7.3 g Mono, 1.8 g Poly, 3.1 g Sat); 33 mg Cholesterol; 34 g Carbohydrate; 1 g Fibre; 3 g Protein; 199 mg Sodium

pumpkin nut cake

The sparkly sugar glaze will catch the eye of anyone with a sweet tooth. Freshly whipped cream, sprinkled with cinnamon, works beautifully with the cake or in the coffee.

Butter (or hard margarine), softened	1/2 cup	125 mL
Granulated sugar	1 cup	250 mL
Brown sugar, packed	1/2 cup	125 mL
Large eggs	2	2
Cooked, mashed pumpkin (or canned pure pumpkin, no spices)	1 cup	250 mL
All-purpose flour	2 cups	500 mL
Chopped pecans, toasted (see Tip, page 64)	1 cup	250 mL
Baking powder	2 tsp.	10 mL
Baking soda	1 tsp.	5 mL
Ground cinnamon	1 tsp.	5 mL
Ground ginger	1/2 tsp.	2 mL
Ground nutmeg	1/2 tsp.	2 mL
Salt	1/4 tsp.	1 mL
Milk	1/2 cup	125 mL

CINNAMON TOPPING

Granulated sugar	2 tbsp.	30 mL
Ground cinnamon	1/2 tsp.	2 mL
Butter (or hard margarine), melted	2 tbsp.	30 mL

Beat first 3 ingredients in large bowl until light and creamy. Add eggs, 1 at a time, beating well after each addition. Add pumpkin. Beat well. Mixture may look slightly curdled.

Combine next 8 ingredients in medium bowl. Add to pumpkin mixture in 3 additions, alternating with milk in 2 additions, beginning and ending with flour mixture. Spread evenly in greased 12 cup (3 L) Bundt pan. Bake in 350°F (175°C) oven for about 45 minutes, until wooden pick inserted in centre of cake comes out clean. Let stand in pan on wire rack for 10 minutes before inverting onto wire rack to cool slightly.

Cinnamon Topping: Combine sugar and cinnamon in small bowl. Brush top of warm cake with melted butter. Sprinkle with cinnamon mixture. Cuts into 16 wedges.

1 wedge: 276 Calories; 13.3 g Total Fat (5.5 g Mono, 1.6 g Poly, 5.4 g Sat); 48 mg Cholesterol; 37 g Carbohydrate; 1 g Fibre; 4 g Protein; 256 mg Sodium

peanut butter marble cake

A box of cake mix provides the speed, while peanut butter and a vanilla glaze add the homemade touch to this delicious Bundt cake variation.

Box of marble cake mix (2 layer size)	1	1
Large eggs	3	3
Water	1 cup	250 mL
Smooth peanut butter	1/3 cup	75 mL
Cooking oil	1/4 cup	60 mL
VANILLA DRIZZLE		
Water	1 tbsp.	15 mL
Vanilla extract	1/4 tsp.	1 mL
Icing (confectioner's) sugar	1 cup	250 mL

Set aside chocolate envelope from cake mix. Combine contents of yellow cake mix pouch and next 4 ingredients in large bowl. Beat for about 2 minutes until smooth. Spread 3/4 of batter evenly in greased and floured 12 cup (3 L) Bundt pan. Add chocolate envelope contents to remaining batter. Mix. Drop by tablespoonfuls over yellow batter. Swirl knife through batter to create marble effect. Bake in 350°F (175°C) oven for 45 to 50 minutes, until wooden pick inserted in centre of cake comes out clean. Let stand in pan on wire rack for 30 minutes. Invert onto serving plate.

Vanilla Drizzle: Stir water and vanilla into icing sugar in small bowl until smooth. Add more icing sugar or water if necessary until barely pourable consistency. Drizzle over warm cake. Cuts into 12 wedges.

1 wedge: 317 Calories; 14.7 g Total Fat (5.2 g Mono, 3.1 g Poly, 2.5 g Sat); 53 mg Cholesterol; 45 g Carbohydrate; 2 g Fibre; 5 g Protein; 272 mg Sodium

sweet nectar cake

If you're planning to freeze this easy cake, glaze it after defrosting so the icing sugar mixture can run down the sides in a tantalizing manner.

Large eggs	4	4
Box of orange cake mix (2 layer size)	1	1
Apricot nectar	1 cup	250 mL
Cooking oil	1/2 cup	125 mL
Box of instant vanilla pudding powder (4-serving size)	1	1

SWEET NECTAR GLAZE		
Apricot nectar	1 tbsp.	15 mL
Icing (confectioner's) sugar	1/2 cup	125 mL

Put first 5 ingredients into large bowl. Beat until smooth. Spread evenly in greased and floured 12 cup (3 L) Bundt pan. Bake in 350°F (175°C) oven for about 50 minutes, until wooden pick inserted in centre of cake comes out clean. Let stand in pan on wire rack for 15 minutes before removing to wire rack to cool.

Sweet Nectar Glaze: Stir nectar into icing sugar in small bowl until smooth. Add more icing sugar or nectar if necessary until barely pourable consistency. Drizzle onto cake. Cuts into 16 wedges.

1 wedge: 256 Calories; 12.1 g Total Fat (7.3 g Mono, 2.6 g Poly, 1.8 g Sat); 54 mg Cholesterol; 35 g Carbohydrate; trace Fibre; 3 g Protein; 151 mg Sodium

pineapple nut coffee cake

Quick breads can be frozen whole, as described on page 34, or as individual pieces—handy for packed lunches or a fast indulgence with an afternoon cup of coffee...or tea!

All-purpose flour	2 1/2 cups	625 mL
Finely chopped walnuts (or pecans)	1 cup	250 mL
Finely chopped glazed pineapple	3/4 cup	175 mL
Baking powder	1 1/2 tsp.	7 mL
Salt	1/2 tsp.	2 mL
Hard margarine (or butter), softened	1 cup	250 mL
Granulated sugar	1 cup	250 mL
Large eggs	5	5
Crushed pineapple, with juice	3/4 cup	175 mL
Brandy extract	2 tsp.	10 mL

Combine first 5 ingredients in large bowl. Make a well in centre.

Beat margarine and sugar in medium bowl until light and creamy. Add in eggs, 1 at a time, beating well after each addition. Add crushed pineapple and extract. Beat. Add to well. Stir until just moistened. Spread evenly in greased 10 inch (25 cm) angel food tube pan. Bake in 275°F (140°C) oven for about 2 hours, until wooden pick inserted in centre of cake comes out clean. Let stand in pan on wire rack for 10 minutes before removing to wire rack to cool. Cuts into 24 wedges.

1 wedge: 232 Calories; 12.8 g Total Fat (6.5 g Mono, 3.2 g Poly, 2.3 g Sat); 45 mg Cholesterol; 27 g Carbohydrate; 1 g Fibre; 4 g Protein; 168 mg Sodium

toasted walnut cake

Let this maple-kissed cake cool in its pan as directed; as with all quickbreads, the rest allows the cake to release steam while holding its shape.

Butter (or hard margarine), softened	1 cup	250 mL
Brown sugar, packed	1 cup	250 mL
Granulated sugar	1 cup	250 mL
Large eggs	4	4
Vanilla extract	1 tsp.	5 mL
All-purpose flour	2 1/2 cups	625 mL
Baking powder	2 tsp.	10 mL
Salt	1/2 tsp.	2 mL
Milk	1 cup	250 mL
Chopped walnuts, toasted (see Tip, page 64)	1 cup	250 mL

MAPLE GLAZE

Icing (confectioner's) sugar	1 cup	250 mL
Maple (or maple-flavoured) syrup	1/4 cup	60 mL
Butter (or hard margarine), softened	2 tsp.	10 mL
Vanilla extract	1/4 tsp.	1 mL
Chopped walnuts, toasted (see Tip, page 64)	2 tbsp.	30 mL

Beat first 3 ingredients in large bowl until light and creamy. Add eggs, 1 at a time, beating well after each addition. Add vanilla. Stir.

Combine next 3 ingredients in medium bowl. Add to butter mixture in 3 additions, alternating with milk in 2 additions, beginning and ending with flour mixture.

Add walnuts. Stir. Spread evenly in greased 10 inch (25 cm) angel food tube pan. Bake in 350°F (175°C) oven for about 1 hour, until wooden pick inserted in centre of cake comes out clean. Let stand in pan on wire rack for 30 minutes before removing to plate.

Maple Glaze: Beat first 4 ingredients in medium bowl until smooth. Makes about 2/3 cup (150 mL) glaze. Drizzle over cake, allowing glaze to drip down side.

Sprinkle with walnuts. Let stand for about 15 minutes until glaze is set. Cuts into 16 wedges.

1 wedge: 420 Calories; 19.5 g Total Fat (5.4 g Mono, 4.2 g Poly, 8.7 g Sat); 89 mg Cholesterol; 57 g Carbohydrate; 1 g Fibre; 7 g Protein; 280 mg Sodium

hermit cake

Fans of hermit cookies will love the classic combination of spices, walnuts and dates served up in a mile-high cake. Serve as is, sprinkle with icing sugar, or top with the Vanilla Drizzle, page 52.

Butter, softened	2 cups	500 mL
Brown sugar, packed	3 cups	750 mL
Large eggs	6	6
Lemon juice	1/3 cup	75 mL
Vanilla extract	4 tsp.	20 mL
All-purpose flour	4 1/2 cups	1.1 L
Chopped pitted dates	3 cups	750 mL
Chopped walnuts	3 cups	750 mL
Baking powder	4 tsp.	20 mL
Ground cinnamon	2 tsp.	10 mL
Salt	1/4 tsp.	1 mL

Beat butter and brown sugar in large bowl until thick and creamy. Add eggs, 1 at a time, beating well after each addition. Add lemon juice and vanilla. Beat well.

Combine remaining 6 ingredients in separate large bowl. Add to butter mixture. Stir well. Spread evenly in greased and floured 10 inch (25 cm) angel food tube pan. Bake in 275°F (140°C) oven for 2 1/2 to 3 hours, until wooden pick inserted in centre of cake comes out clean. Let stand in pan on wire rack for 10 minutes before removing to wire rack to cool. Cuts into 24 wedges.

1 wedge: 525 Calories; 28.0 g Total Fat (7.5 g Mono, 7.3 g Poly, 11.4 g Sat); 98 mg Cholesterol; 65 g Carbohydrate; 3 g Fibre; 7 g Protein; 224 mg Sodium

recipe index

topical tips

Making soured milk: If a recipe calls for soured milk, measure 1 tbsp. (15 mL) white vinegar or lemon juice into a 1 cup (250 mL) liquid measure. Add enough milk to make 1 cup (250 mL). Stir. Let stand for one minute.

Quick breads explained: All baking needs some kind of leavening agent to make it rise. Traditional yeast-based breads can take several hours from start to finish. Batters made with baking powder or soda go into the oven much faster, which is why they're called quick breads.

Toasting nuts, seeds or coconut: Cooking times will vary for each ingredient, so never toast them together. For small amounts, place ingredient in an ungreased frying pan. Heat on medium for three to five minutes, stirring often, until golden. For larger amounts, spread ingredient evenly in an ungreased shallow pan. Bake in a 350°F (175°C) oven for five to 10 minutes, stirring or shaking often, until golden.

Zest first; juice second: When a recipe calls for grated zest and juice, it's easier to grate the lemon or lime first, then juice it. Be careful not to grate down to the pith (white part of the peel), which is bitter and best avoided.

Nutrition Information Guidelines

Each recipe is analyzed using the Canadian Nutrient File from Health Canada, which is based on the United States Department of Agriculture (USDA) Nutrient Database.

- If more than one ingredient is listed (such as "butter or hard margarine"), or if a range is given (1 – 2 tsp., 5 – 10 mL), only the first ingredient or first amount is analyzed.

- For meat, poultry and fish, the serving size per person is based on the recommended 4 oz. (113 g) uncooked weight (without bone), which is 2 – 3 oz. (57 – 85 g) cooked weight (without bone) — approximately the size of a deck of playing cards.

- Milk used is 1% M.F. (milk fat), unless otherwise stated.

- Cooking oil used is canola oil, unless otherwise stated.

- Ingredients indicating "sprinkle," "optional" or "for garnish" are not included in the nutrition information.

- The fat in recipes and combination foods can vary greatly depending on the sources and types of fats used in each specific ingredient. For these reasons, the count of saturated, monounsaturated and polyunsaturated fats may not add up to the total fat content.